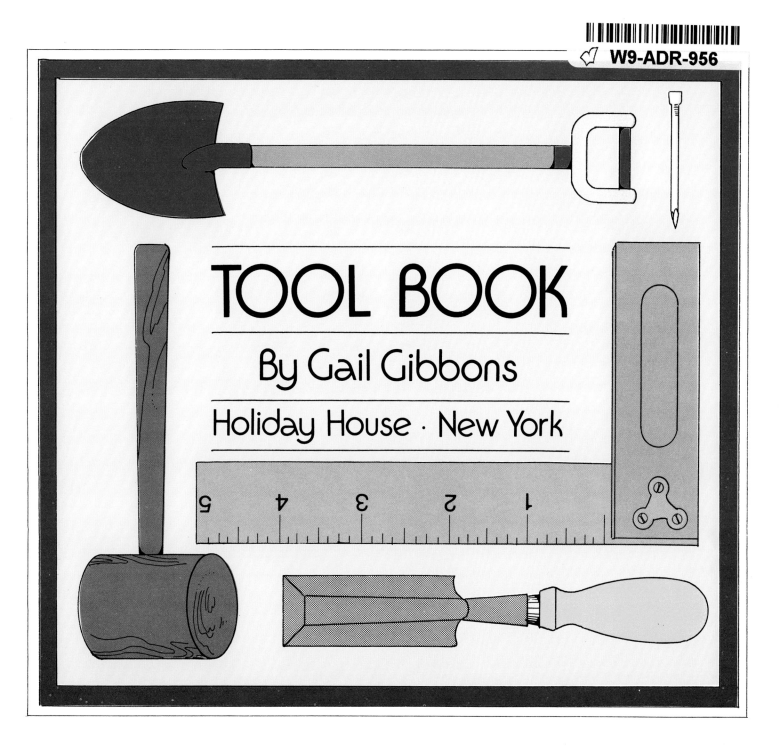

TOOL BOOK

By Gail Gibbons

Holiday House · New York

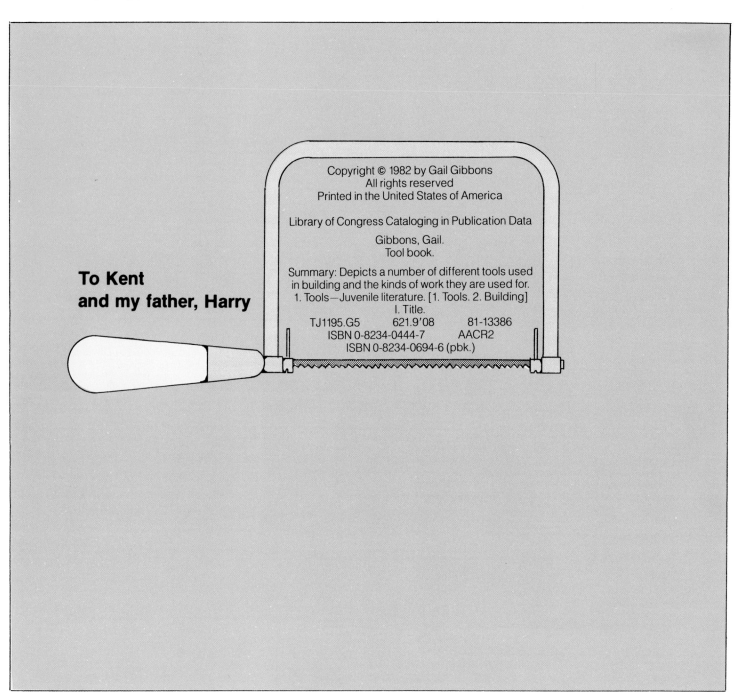

**To Kent
and my father, Harry**

Copyright © 1982 by Gail Gibbons
All rights reserved
Printed in the United States of America

Library of Congress Cataloging in Publication Data

Gibbons, Gail.
Tool book.

Summary: Depicts a number of different tools used
in building and the kinds of work they are used for.
1. Tools—Juvenile literature. [1. Tools. 2. Building]
I. Title.
TJ1195.G5   621.9'08   81-13386
ISBN 0-8234-0444-7   AACR2
ISBN 0-8234-0694-6 (pbk.)

Tools help us build.

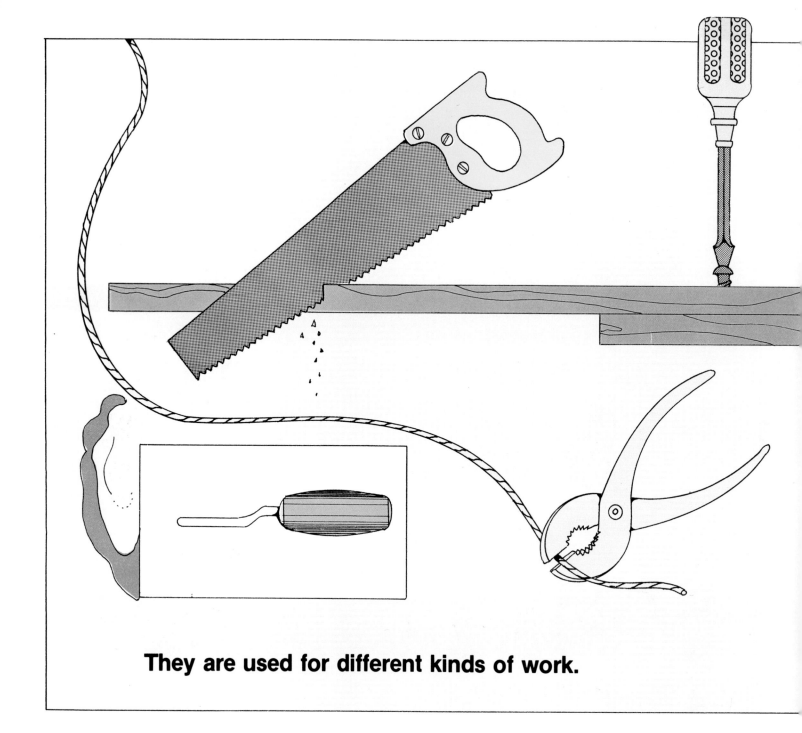

They are used for different kinds of work.

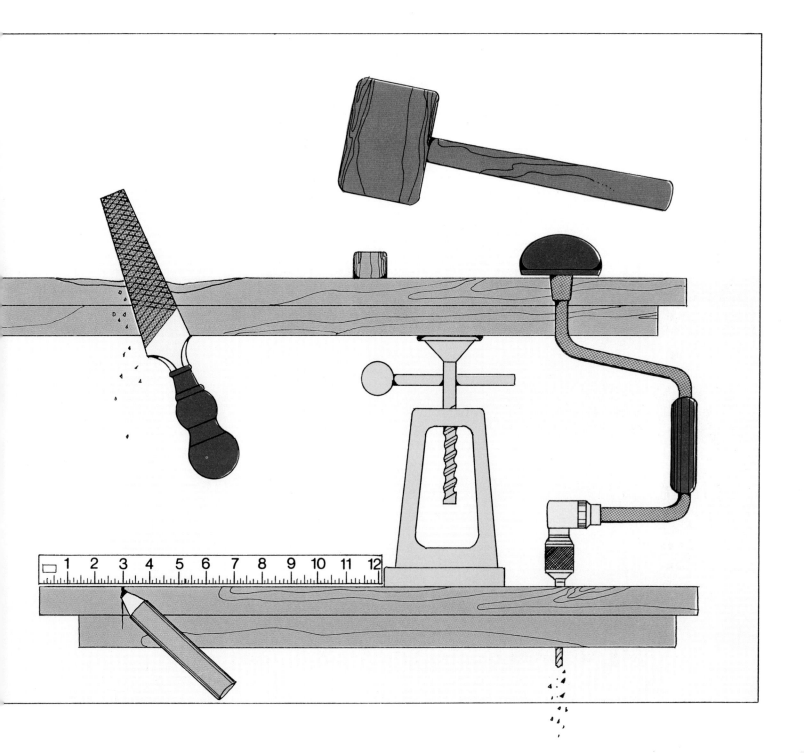

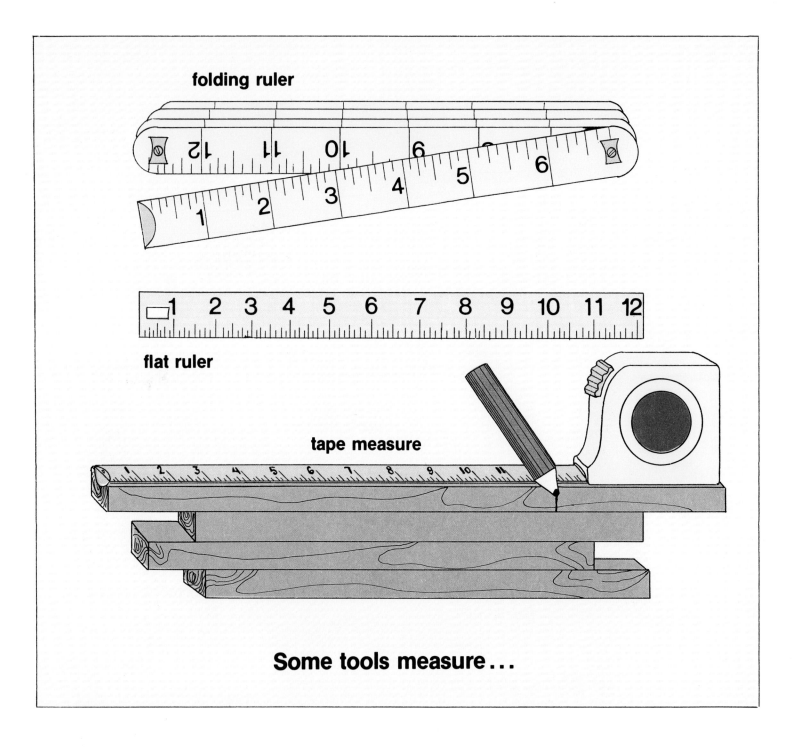

folding ruler

flat ruler

tape measure

Some tools measure . . .

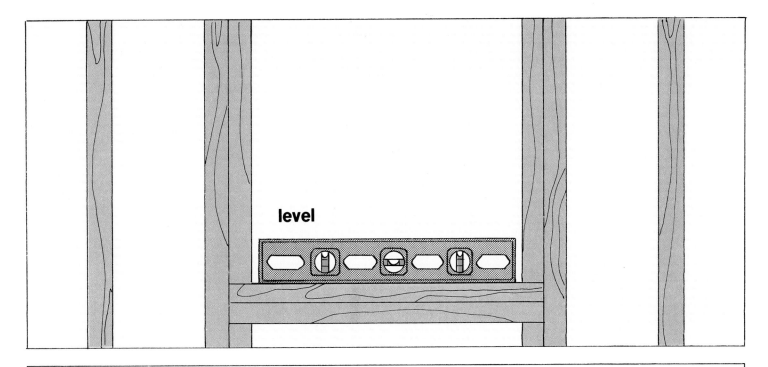

level

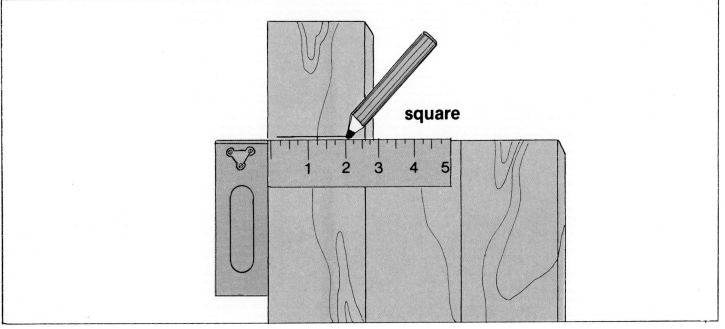

square

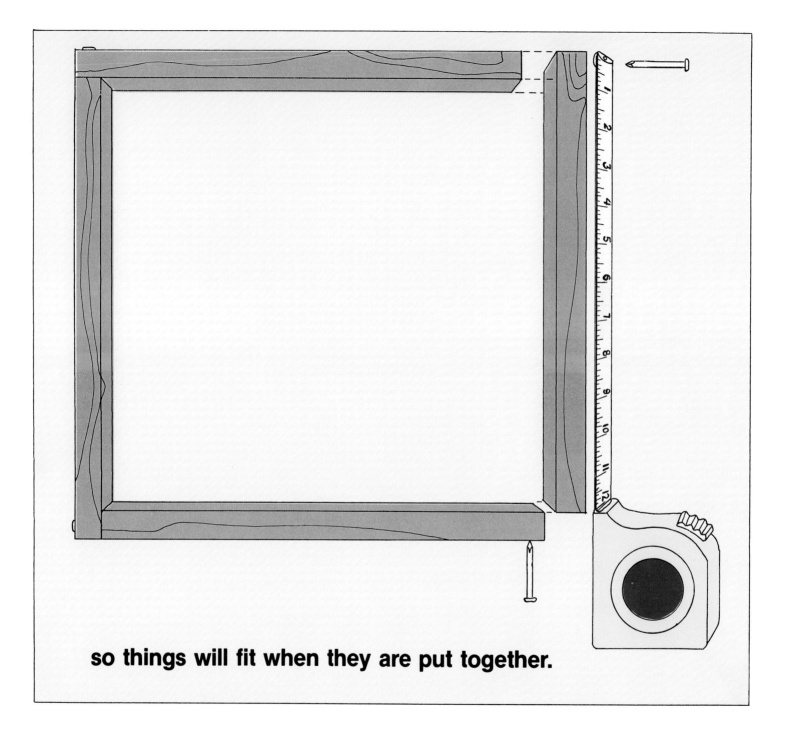

so things will fit when they are put together.

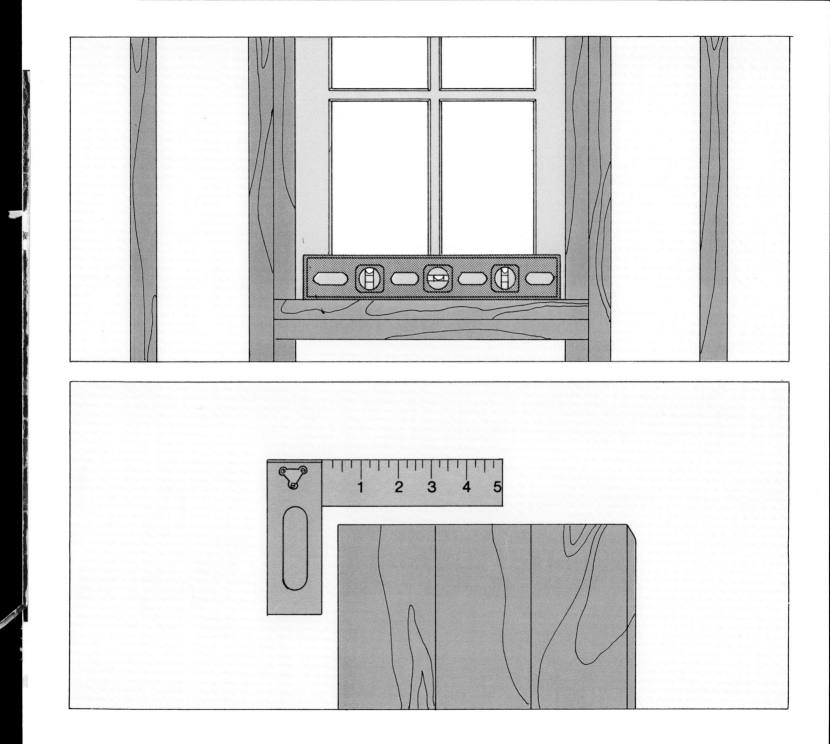

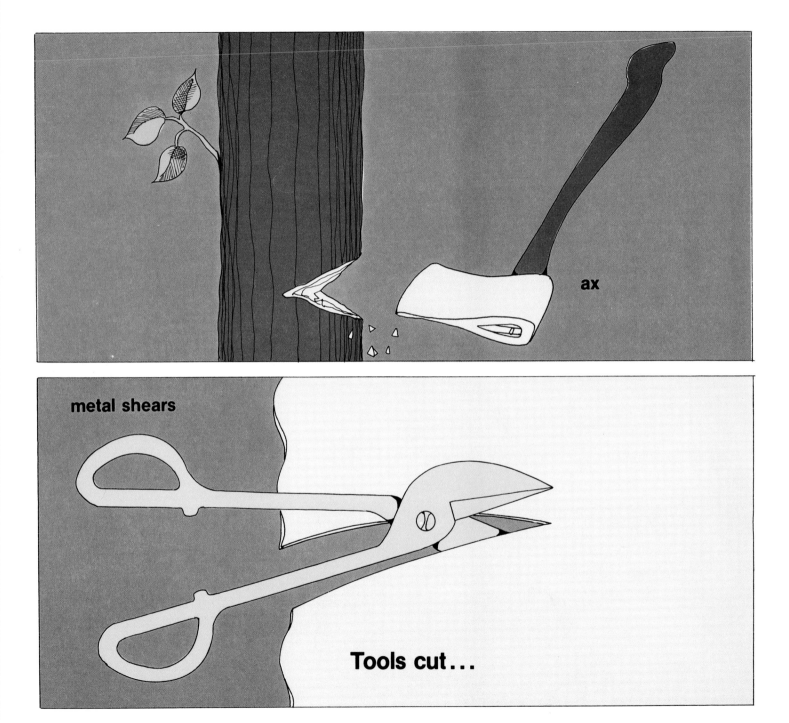

ax

metal shears

Tools cut...

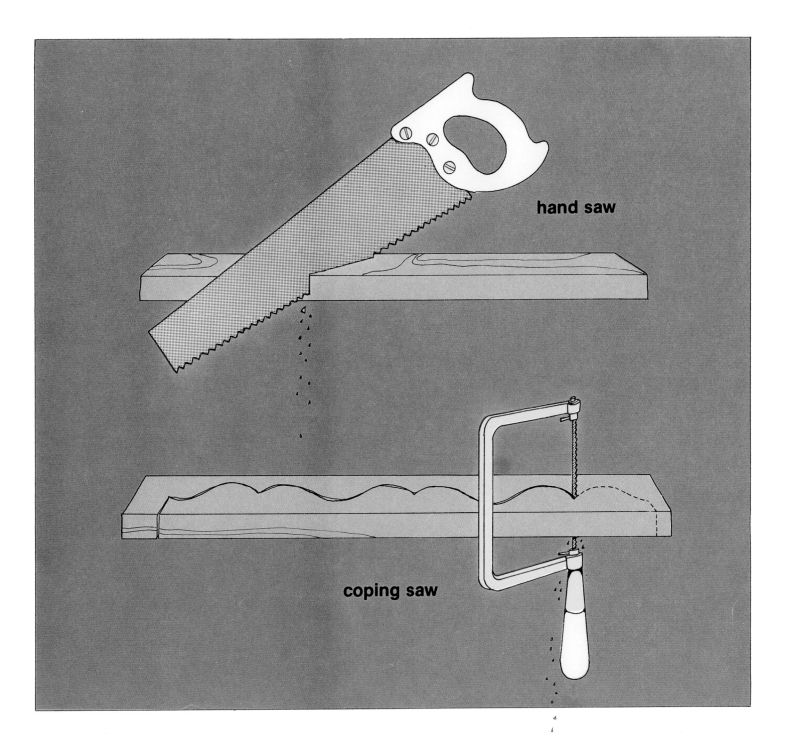

hand saw

coping saw

plane

scrape and shape...

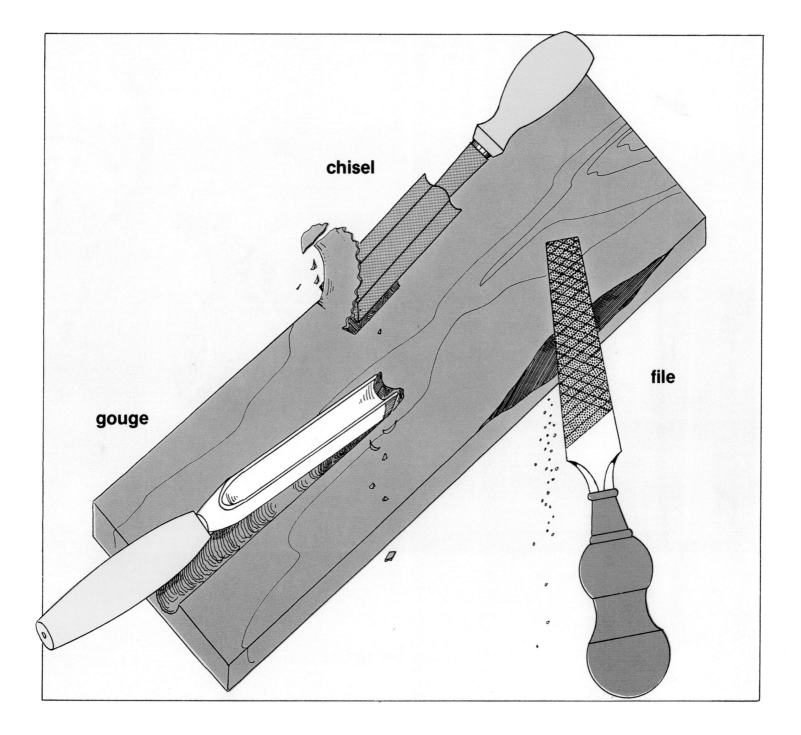

gouge

chisel

file

hammer

and pound.

sledge hammer

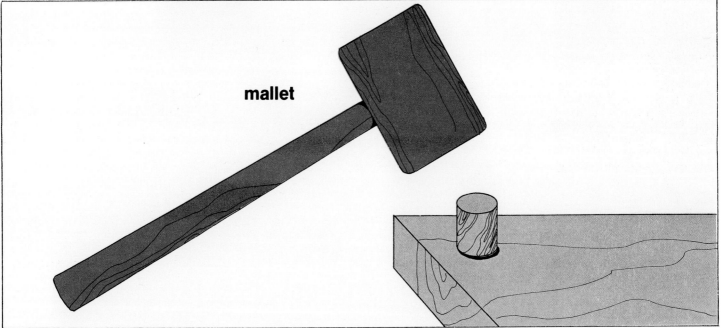

mallet

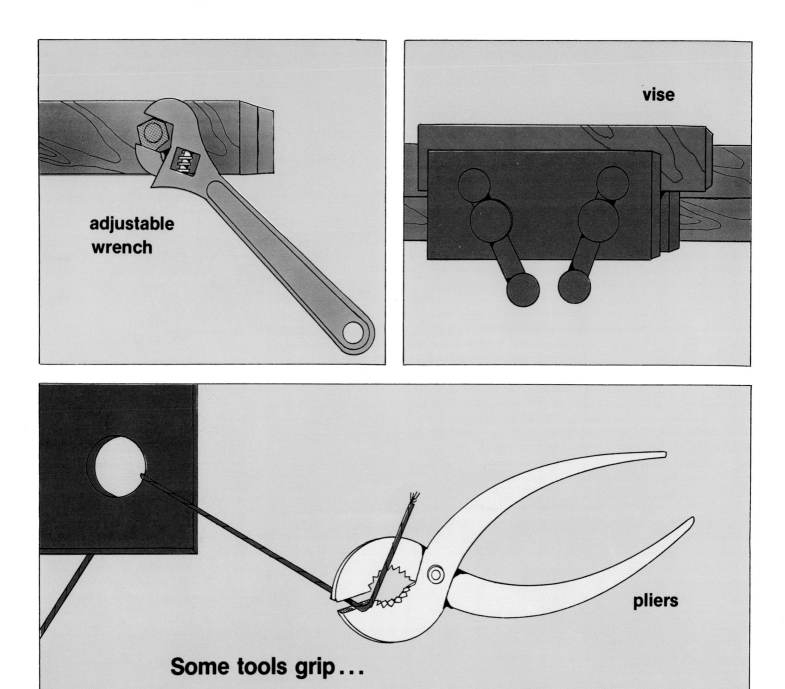

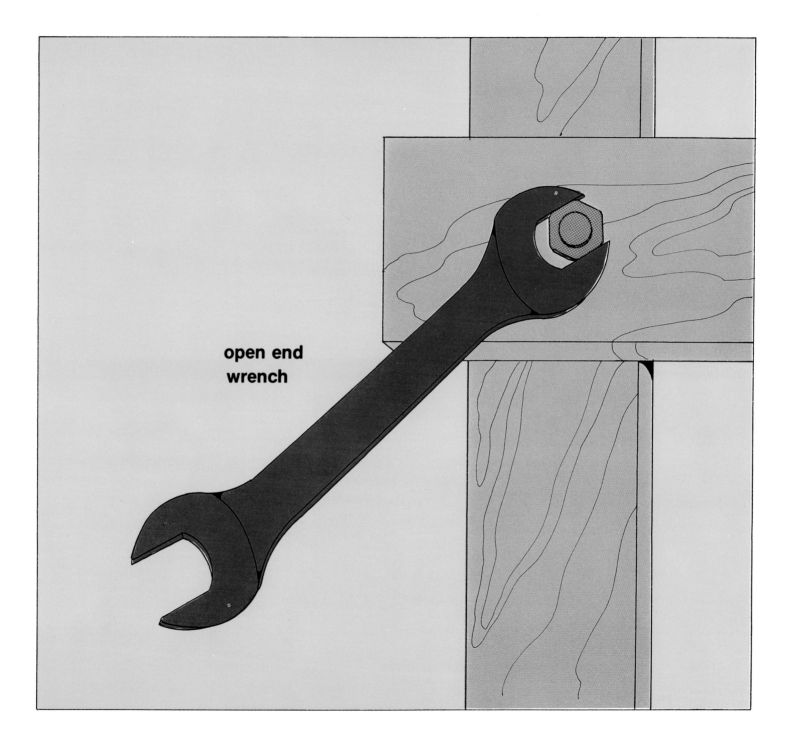

**open end
wrench**

shovel

and others make holes.

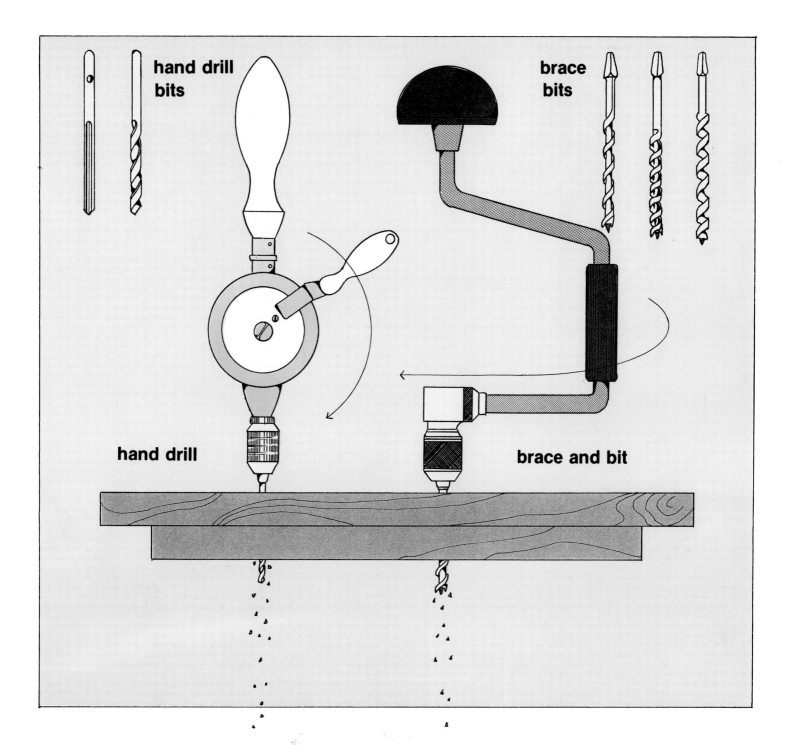

hand drill
bits

brace
bits

hand drill

brace and bit

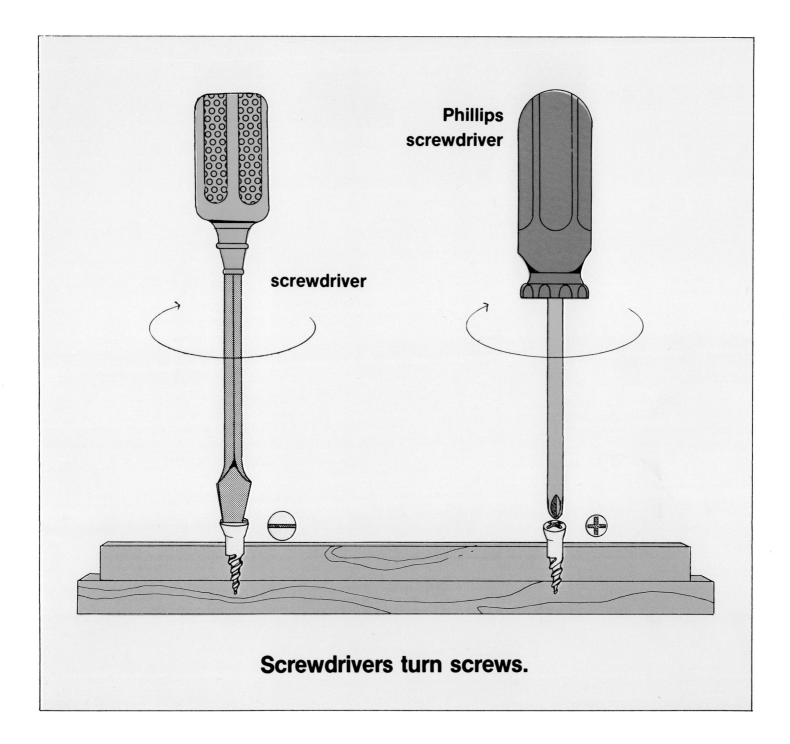

Phillips screwdriver

screwdriver

Screwdrivers turn screws.

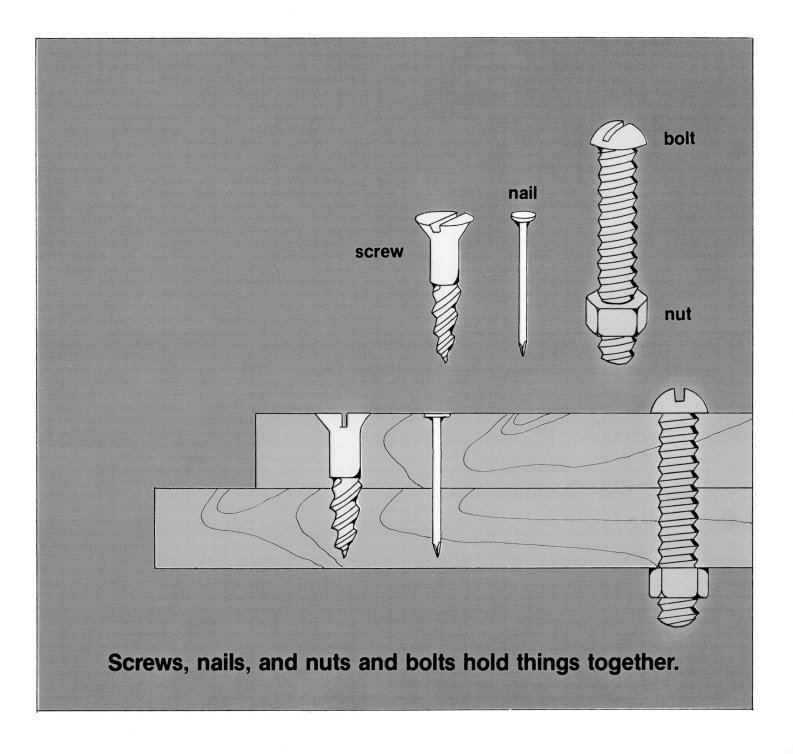

screw   **nail**   **bolt**   **nut**

Screws, nails, and nuts and bolts hold things together.

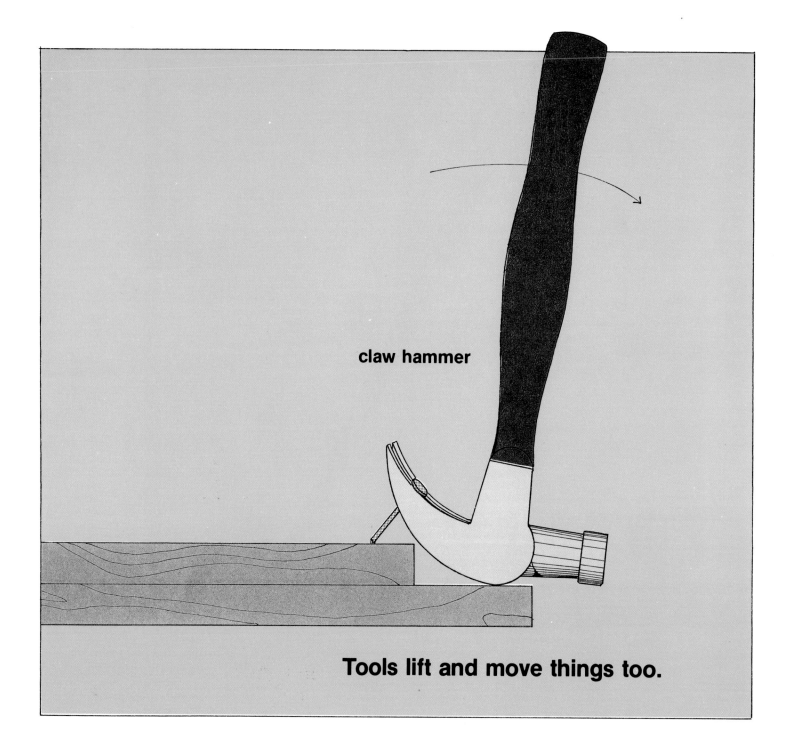

claw hammer

Tools lift and move things too.

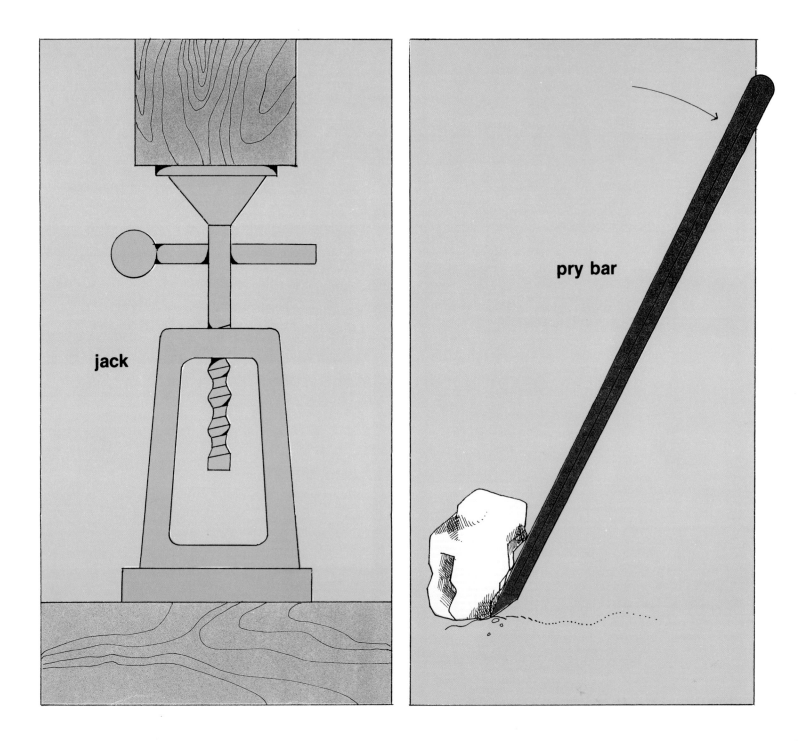

jack

pry bar

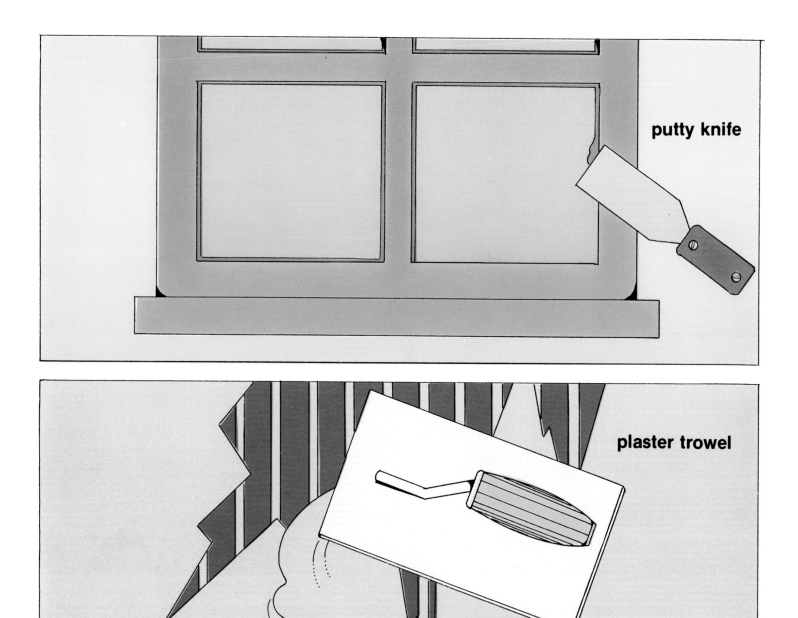

putty knife

plaster trowel

Others are used to help cover surfaces.

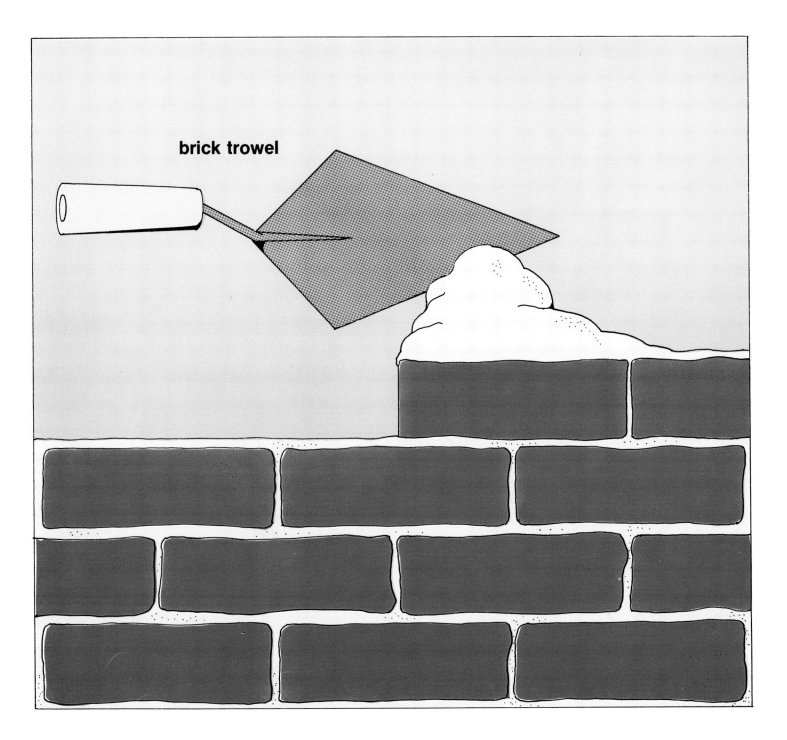

brick trowel

Tools are put away in a tool box...

or hung on a wall to keep them in order...

near the workbench.

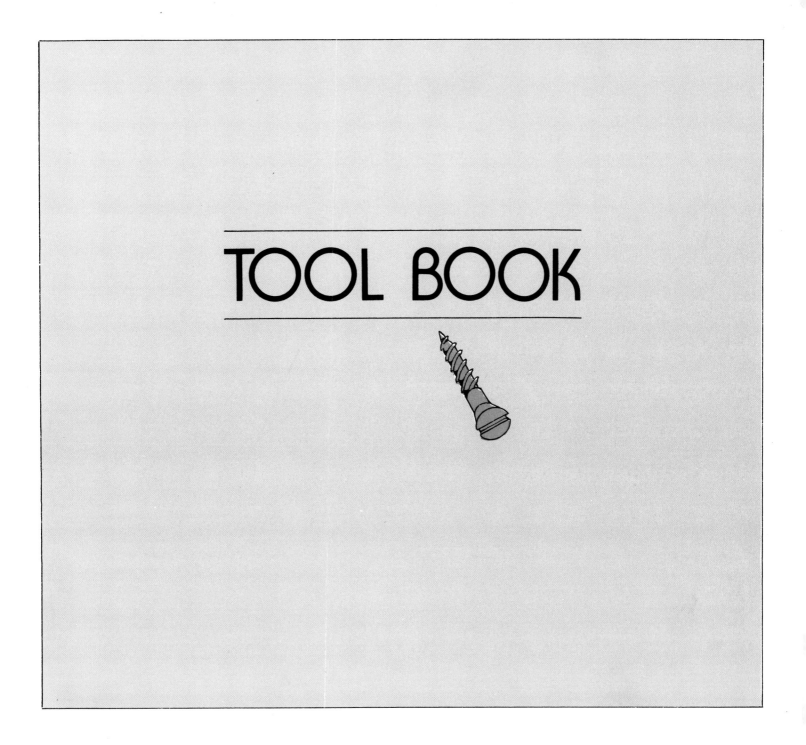

TOOL BOOK